T0132050

Finding My Spark & Keeping It

MARGARET COAN

Balboa Press books may be ordered through booksellers or by contacting:

Balboa Press
A Division of Hay House
1663 Liberty Drive
Bloomington, IN 47403
www.balboapress.com
844-682-1282

Interior Image Credit: Margaret Coan

ISBN: 979-8-7652-3687-1 (sc)
ISBN: 979-8-7652-3688-8 (e)

Library of Congress Control Number: 2023901725

Print information available on the last page.

Balboa Press rev. date: 01/30/2023

BALBOA.PRESS
A DIVISION OF HAY HOUSE

Dedication

To
John
Love of my life
Michael
Music of my heart
Patrick
Silence of my soul
Ryan
Dance of my spirit

I dedicate these pages to my amazing family who never gave up on me even though I had given up on myself. To my ex-husband who was determined that I find my spark again, who loved me as I had never been loved before. To our three sons who each loved me with all they had, who believed in me even though I had no belief in myself.

It was the daily active love of these four beautiful men and all the prayers and love I was receiving from many others that inspired me to Find My Spark Again; to choose to live, feel and love again.

Words can never express the deep deep deep GRATITUDE I WILL ALWAYS HOLD IN MY HEART AND SOUL for all this LOVE that saved me.

I pray this story may bring the spark back to another's life. I hope these words will encourage the reader to never give up on the power of love, the power of prayer, and the TRUTH that with God All Things are possible.

My Son's Request

It all began with my son's request, and this white blank page that is inviting me to create a living story, crafted in my experience, A gleaming blank page that I hope will open into a book of truth, hope and promise.

Three years ago I emerged from a suffocating darkness into a new wondrous light. My sons have encouraged me to share my experience, with the hope that it might help others who have found themselves at the bottom of a black deep well, with no known way out.

I am now ready to put my experience of suicidal depression on paper. I now understand how I got there, how I got out, and how I know I will never go there again..

Yes. I have found My Spark and am Keeping It, thanks to the amazing love of my ex-husband John and our three sacred sons Michael, Patrick and Ryan and all the prayers and love of so many. My heart knows the transforming power of True Love. My soul knows that all life is created by a living, breathing Divine Creator who ignites every sunrise and every sunset, who heals every wound, who dries every tear, who longs for each of us to know how much we have always been and always will be loved.

I am beginning to wonder if these moments of tormenting darkness, these moments of being broken wide open, are when new life is being born and we don't know it yet?. Could it be like a winter that opens into spring? My experience tells me my darkness birthed a brilliant new light in my heart and in my life. My long dark winter has opened into brilliant blossoms of wondrous spring. My hope is that in sharing my simple experience you too, will find Your Spark and Keep It!!!

The Beginning

I danced into my life, the youngest of four. Golden curls swirling in the light of my days, as I shared my unedited joy to all around me. I moved in the world like a dandelion puff, free and easy in the warm sandy dunes and frolicking waves, open and curious.

My father called me Imp, my mother, Polly while my birth certificate named me Margaret. I was never called Meg or Peggy for my sister and mother were already wearing those names.

My days were filled with simple joys chasing butterflies, dancing with cows and flying on swings. Life was a wonderful adventure and nature a fantastic playground.

My family spent the summer in Rhode Island where I dove in the salty waves and rolled in the hot soft sand with my summer friends. These magical summer days were laced with sunfish sailing, water skiing, open jeep riding, tie dying, and painting. My outer world danced in joy while inside, behind closed doors pulsed another world of dark fears, which I learned at a very young age, to hide from myself and everyone around me. I crafted so many lies to keep me afloat in the rip tides of trauma.

Hidden Truths

My mothers battle with Manic Depression, carved my soul with deep gashing wounds. Wounds that I was taught to hide, pretend were not there, to put on a happy face, to never talk about, and most especially never feel the magnitude of the experiences!!! Her mania would erupt in volcanic impressions. I never knew if it was going to be a good day or an explosive day. I never knew what landscape I was going to walk into as I slid out of bed.. I never knew, so I walked on egg shells and learned to run and hide. I learned to suffocate my feelings and pretend they were not there. I created imaginary worlds to take me out of the one i was living.

I carried these heavy wounds into the rest of my life, where they painted my future experiences of continued pain and suffering. I carried bags of lies that my experience taught me, and I believed with all my heart and soul; that I was a cry baby, that I needed to grow up, that I was fat, stupid and ugly, that my sister was better than me, that she was prettier, smarter, and more loved. I carried jealousy, anger, rage, rejection, failure, less than, not good enough; all inner mantras that were creating my experience, yet I was pretending they were not there. I was choosing to lie to myself, for I believed all these lies were my protection, my safe haven, and yet I have learned they are the cause of all my unloving choices and all my unloving experiences.

Shock Waves

Upon returning home from a weekend with my best friend, I walked into our house and could feel a darkness so thick it was a challenge to walk up the stairs to my parents room where I found Mom lying in bed with a blank stare. Her body was there, yet it was crystal clear she was somewhere else. I desperately tried to connect to her, to take away the blank, empty, heavy space that surrounded her. I told her about my weekend, I gave her a hug, I longed for a smile, a hello, anything. All that was there was a blank empty stare. I desperately longed for a way to connect to her, but all the lines were closed. The person I loved the most, the person who I adored, the person who I thought loved me, was gone. The darkness I felt when entering our home, was lying in my Mothers bed, a blank empty stare... I sat watching, hoping, waiting, longing for my Mom to return.

Later that night, as I lay in my bed curled in fear, I heard commotion in my parents room, and the next morning I woke up to unexpected desperation. Mom was gone. She had been whisked away in the dark of night. The bed she had been laying in just yesterday, was empty, cold, tucked in sheets were all that was left. I could barely breathe for the air was thick, wet, dark emptiness. Questions upon questions spiraled through my eleven year old mind. Where was Mom? Who had taken her? Why was she gone? Was she ok? Would she be back? Was she safe? Was she being taken care of? Why? Why? Why? Would this deep bone pain of not knowing ever stop throbbing? Would this trembling fear ever stop pulsing? Would my world ever spin in unedited joy again?

The Visit

I was eleven and my brother 12, as we held hands with Dad walking down a long dark hallway, up dark brown wooden stairs and into Moms room. As we turned the corner into her room my life changed forever. This was the first of many breakdowns my mother would have, locked in a mental institution that understood nothing of her pain, understood nothing of how she landed there, understood nothing, and tried to help her in so many unkind and unloving ways. Medications, straps, forcing, prodding, probing, to stop her from expressing her rage, that became manic depression rather than bone deep grief for all the ways she had not been loved, for all the ways she did not even understand what love was, for all the ways she believed so many lies of her own and of my father. My Mothers struggles with the demons of mental illness, carved an experience that has driven my life in all so many ways, some life affirming while others life destroying.

As the youngest in the family I became my mothers ray of hope, until she had no hope left and took her life three days after my twenty third birthday. A moment whose impact was so piercing, I am just now, 44 years later, finally grieving and healing this devastating loss of my Mom, who I always adored. Grieving that I had absolutely NO IDEA what love was. That my concepts of love were completely distorted and confused in my childhood experiences.

My mother who struggled with the many demons of manic depression used me as her psychiatric aid, used me to feel loved, used me to make her happy. I took on this task with all my heart and soul and when she took her life I knew for certain I was a failure, for I blamed myself for her deep, deep, deep sadness, that I tried so very very hard to take away with my love.

I have learned that my fear of feeling this great complicated loss, created a very similar experience in my life. I have learned what we do not feel, what we choose to hide inside of us, runs us the rest of our lives as we try to fill all our fears of loss with unloving demanding addictions. The saddest Truth I have learned is that very few people on earth have any idea what True Love is, all we know is conditional, demanding, controlling, barter that we believe to be love; you do for me then I will do for you. If you do not do what I want I wont do anything you want; it is actually extremely unloving and cruel and yet earthlings call this kind of relationship love, even though time and again it hurts and creates so much suffering and pain.

I have learned True Love never has any pain or suffering. True Love is everlasting and eternal and NOTHING can ever destroy it. I have learned True Love endures, is patient, is kind, is compassionate, understanding and always Truthful. I have learned that grief is a result of not knowing anything about love. That grief comes when we feel that we were not loved, but instead used and often abused. I have learned that grief is how we forgive and repent, how we are purified, how our souls heal. Indeed, as our youngest son reminds me, "you must feel to heal". May sound so very trite, and even like a hallmark card sentiment, and yet, I have experienced the profound Truth, in this very simple statement. A now healthy mantra I remember whenever I feel hurt by another's choice or my own. It actually is in our choices to not feel that we create our suffering and pain, for we hold it in, lie to ourselves, lie to others, become resentful, bitter, hateful, angry, rigid, jealous; all creations in all our unloving choices. To fight against another's hurt, to seek vengeance rather than forgiveness. We stay in our rigid closed hard shells of unending lies and continue to create more and more suffering and pain. We are like hamsters in a cage going around and around, making the same choices, and expecting different results; the definition of insanity, for certain, yet we believe it is the way to happiness. We do not want to take responsibility for our choices, instead, we usually choose to blame others, blame ourselves, or blame God.

I was an expert actress, for I had mastered looking happy, when the Truth inside of me was a vastly different landscape, a drastically different story, which was orchestrating my life, my choices. Fear was the conductor in the symphony of my living, and the results were full of gut wrenching, skin peeling pain, for I had put my Faith in the Fear of my experience, rather than in the Truth and Love of our Divine Creator God.

Shattered

Some experiences in life shatter us so deeply our lives will always bear the marks. Some experiences are so gut wrenching we try to run and hide from the pain. We build a wall of wishful, fantasy thinking, a wall of false hope, a wall of lies, when in that moment lives no hope. When in that moment pulses the rhythm of deep dark despair. We run so hard from the pain of the experience believing we will be set free, only to learn years later, the experience is the fuel of our future pain. In our desperate fear and desire to not feel the bone piercing pain we are destined to recreate a similar story until we finally decide to feel in order to heal. Rather than plunge into the journey of grief that is designed to free our pain and suffering we believe being strong means not feeling, when the Truth is real strength is born in opening our hearts wide open to feel every single moment of our experience, all of it, including all the pain of our childhoods we are all hiding from.

Each time Mom left us, left me, a little piece of my heart was chipped away. Each time I chose hope, I chose to believe my love for her would make her happy, I chose to visit her so she would know she was not alone. The days I visited she and her friends called it Polly day and I really treasured those moments. I was always happy to see my Mom and know she was ok, yet at the same time, I missed her so badly. At the same time I wished she could have been home with us. I wished she was happy, really that was my only wish, it was so hard to watch her suffer, so impossible to understand. The more Mom suffered, the sicker she got in her manic moments, the more I learned to hide, pretend, to myself and everyone around me. The landscape of my family was laced with constant unexpected and feared outbreaks of anger between my parents. My childhood was a battle ground of sides, Moms or Dads, I chose Moms, my older sister chose Dads and my brothers chose the middle. While each of us lived in the same house, how it infected and impacted our lives is completely unique. We each were deeply wounded yet how we have managed those wounds is all wrapped up in our individual choices and experiences.

Call For Help

It was a hot, sweaty, wet, summer day in Boston. I had just arrived back into the city a few days before from leaving my husband in Maine, and returning home to begin again. I was living with my Dad when the phone rang and I was told Mom was at home in her apartment, she had been released from Boston State Hospital. My heart was torn, a part of me really did not want to go and another part of me put one foot in front of the other and knocked on her door. I was stunned by who opened the door, a version of Mom I was seeing for the first time, shacking, bone thin, tattered and torn by her months in captivity. She welcomed me in and we made our way to her small, round kitchen table where we sat. She was drinking coffee, smoking cigarettes and talking to her voices. I desperately searched for how to help. I told her we needed to find a place for her to live where she would not be alone, I told her I would come over the next day to help her with her finances and get her life back on track. We chatted for a while and I left, hugging her and telling her I would see her tomorrow.

Last Call

July 23, the next day, I called Mom to say I could not come over and was shocked when my father answered her phone. I asked him "what are you doing at Mom's?" and he said "your mother is dead ". At that moment, her words she had said to me the day before spiraled through my heart and mind "Pol, I do not have the energy any more". I knew she had taken her life, though the coroner said it was a heart attack, my father said we would not have an autopsy, for I know he knew she had taken her entire bottle of Lithium, a very toxic medication. As I write these words on the page, tears stream down my face, I am still feeling the aftershocks of that moment in my life.

Guilt, shame, blame, and self hatred were carved into my heart at that moment for I had failed at my job as her "psychiatric aid" for that is what she called me. My love was not enough to save her. At that moment, i went into deep, deep, deep hiding and at her funeral I did not shed a tear, in fact, I went to school and closed a huge part of me that I am finally feeling and healing. The deep bone grief of losing the person I loved the most in the world, my Mom. The grief of watching her suffer for so many years. The grief of feeling how my experience taught me love was a one way street, you give, and give and give and even then it is never enough.

Her death became a family secret, no one even admitted she took her own life, for shame suffocated the TRUTH, yet my heart and soul knew for she had told me the day before, she had said goodbye to me when she said "I don't have the energy anymore..."

Six years later I asked my Dad and he finally told the truth. She had taken her life, it felt so good to know I could trust my heart to know the Truth, which is something I continue to learn each and every day.

Guilt

One of the parts of me I hid the most was the part that felt relieved Mom was gone, I still feel so guilty even saying that, for I truly loved my Mom, yet I did not love the burden it put on my life. I did not love feeling it was my job to take care of her, that it was my job to be her psychiatric aid. Though I never felt it was a job, I truly enjoyed going to visit her and her friends at the hospital. What was so hard though was feeling her life was in my hands. My father never visited her when she was in the hospital and in fact I was the only family member that did on any regular schedule mostly because I was the youngest and at home.

I lied to myself about so many things just to get by and avoid feeling the gut wrenching grief of Moms loss. I remember watching kids with their Moms and wishing it was me. I remember watching my daughter in law with her Mom on her wedding day and wishing my Mom had been at my day with my husband John, who never met my Mom, though I know she knows him so well, and loves him so much.

I believe I am able to feel this grief now, for my heart has been opened again and I feel my Mom is healed and well. She is so joyous and happy and showers me with her love each and every day. She tells me how sorry she is for how she hurt us all so badly in her choice to take her life and she knows how it has impacted all our lives so deeply. She and my Dad have reconciled and forgiven each other, and have been encouraging me to forgive them so my life can be free of all that excruciating pain I have been carrying all my life, and they both are so so sorry. Knowing that Mom is well and happy makes me so full of such profound joy. Knowing that she and Dad have made amends makes me so happy, for that is all I ever wanted growing up. They are not partners anymore for they are not soul mates, but they are dear friends and have repented for all the ways they hurt each other and their children in all their lies and unloving choices.

Consequences

It should come as no surprise, yet of course it surely did, to me and to my family, that I would end up curled up in bed for 5 long years, battling with my own demons, stuck in the torments of self hatred, self punishment, self blame after my husband of 35 years told me he saw nothing good in me and left our marriage. Like the day I called my Mom and was told she was dead, when my husband took off his wedding ring, my life, and all its dreams, came to a screeching halt. I cried some very deep tears yet I also did what I had always learned to do, continue on, be "strong", to lie to myself, to hide how angry I really was at life, at my experience, at my husband, for abandoning me, breaking our promise to each other, blaming me for his unhappiness, which I also did too. I believed God would get me through this. I believed that I would not sink under this once again abandonment and betrayal. I believed if I just prayed hard enough my husband would return and my life would be ok again. Instead, I lost any faith I had, or maybe I never really had, for happy endings, for fulfilled dreams. I lost my faith in love, I lost my faith in goodness, I lost my faith in anything good and spiraled into a well of slimy darkness that wanted me to take my life. I believed I was the worst person in this world, and everyone would be so much happier if I left the stage. I know for certain, my husband could not wait to get me out of our house, and out of his life. Unfortunately, I had made him my God, and when he had not interest in me anymore, when he hated me, blamed me, rejected me, and in fact, could not even look me in the eye, my world collapsed into a million sharp edged pieces of blazing hurt, which I was struggling so desperately to NOT feel. I was terrified and wrapped myself in blankets of self punishment and blame for all the ways my life was once again changed in an unexpected moment of someone else's decision to leave and abandon me.

Existence

Each and every day getting out of bed to go to the bathroom felt like carrying hundreds of pounds of boulders, sometimes I literally crawled on all fours. All I wanted to do was sleep, run away, escape the thousands of pounds of guilt, shame, blame that was pulsing through every vein, every tissue of my being. I was delusional and believed I was obese as I lay losing weight each and every day, for I had no interest in eating, for I had no interest in living. I had visions of laying naked in a city park, handcuffed to a bench, it was ice cold winter, and people were throwing knives at me. I believed this was my eternal hell, for all the ways I had failed, all the ways I had disappointed everyone, all the ways I could never be good enough. The guilt was like a wrench I was living inside. I knew I was hurting our children, and that pain was beyond excruciating. John would occasional come in my room and say "your children need you" and those words were like a sharp burning blade cutting through my heart, for I knew he was right, and I also knew, I did not want to feel anymore pain, I could not feel that my mother abandoned us when she took her life, I could not feel that my father abandoned my mother when she was at her darkest hour, I could not feel that my husband abandoned me the exact same way, in my darkest hour, he chose to be with another woman, as I lay crumbled under the dirty sheets. I spent my days searching for ways to escape, yet, the voices of Truth and Love told me there was no escape. That if I took my life my darkness would only get darker. I feel this voice was from my mother and father who knew their choices were in great part why I was in the condition I was in. The hope they had was they knew I believed in life after death. They knew I believed life never ends. So when they told me if I tried to take my life I would just be creating more pain and suffering for all so many, including myself, they had great hope I would believe them and know that there was no way out. Yet I still hoped for one, so I figured if I just kept not eating eventually I might just die, which I crazily believed would be a relief. Thanks to my ex-husbands commitment to me finding my spark again, and our sons enduring love, and prayers from so many, and God's Love and Grace, I am here to share this story, hoping it might help another in their time of darkness, so they too, will find the light. My family never gave up on me, though I had clearly given up on myself. Many family and friends were praying for me, and I know that it was all this love in action, that gave me a chance to find my spark again, to live my life again, to wake up to many Truths I now was ready to learn.

One of the hardest things about sharing this story is knowing how many people I hurt in my unexpressed anger at life, at my parents, at my husband, and even at God for creating a world full of so much suffering and pain. I know that our sons and my ex-husband suffered very much too, and it was because I did not want to take responsibility for what was inside of me. I had spent my life lying to myself about so many things. I had spent my life believing what others had said about me, other people felt about me, most especially my mom, who did not want a fourth child, so even in the womb I felt unwanted, not good enough. I had been on a spiritual journey, had even written a book about Sacred Listening, yet I did not want to listen to my own heart, listen to the pain that had always been a part of my experience.

My parents, and the world around me, taught me so many lies. That I had to earn love, that in order to be loved I had to do things the way others wanted me to do them. My two older brothers constantly told me I was fat, stupid, and ugly, which unfortunately I have always believed. They told me to grow up, stop crying, for I came into the world very sensitive. Over time, like most of us, I learned to stop being me, for being me was wrong, bad, not good enough.

My mothers struggles with her demons of manic depression created a very unpredictable and volatile environment. I never knew what her mood was going to be, and thus, the environment around us. It was like learning to walk on eggshells, trying so hard to not ignite the fires of her uncontrollable rage, which usually she projected towards my father, whose irresponsibility with money, clearly drove her crazy. When she was "well" she was my favorite person to be with. Down to earth, kind, and generous. There was a realness to her I always loved, while my father was more aloof, bossy and controlling. The problem was since I was eleven years old she often was not well. She was often not able to be an active part of my life. She was either busy in her political endeavors, or sick in bed, or away at a hospital . I became her caretaker at this very young age, and now, 57 years later, I understand in my heart it was never my responsibility to take care of her, it was hers, and when she took her life it was not my fault, it was her choice, for like me she believed the world would be better without her.

I remember all these days, one after the other, wrapped in a veil of tormenting gray, no joy, no sorrow, a vast landscape of empty nothingness, indeed, no life. It was like being at a banquet with no way to enjoy any of its offerings. I remember the required walks, food, and outings that all felt like an insurmountable mountain, others wanted me to climb, while I had absolutely no interest in even taking a small step. I was living in the hells of hopelessness, guilt, shame, blame and overwhelming self hatred.

One day that still pierces my heart, my husband at the time, brought our middle son Patrick with him to bring me to the doctors. They came into the room I was staying, with Starbucks teas and coffees, and Patricks huge gorgeous brown eyes looked at me with such hope, such faith that I would get well, and I just sat there knowing I was giving nothing back. He then wrote me the most beautiful letter saying he knew I was going to get well, he knew I would get through this, and that he loved me, and I knew I had no love to give back. The pain of not being able to answer his longing for me to be well, his look, as he sat across from me at the doctors office, still sears my heart. Guilt, self punishment were suffocating me in torment, as I lay under the sheets. I did not want anyone to see me, for I knew they would see how horrible I really was. I looked out the window, watching our neighbors wishing I could be like them. I wish I could be "myself" again. Who was I now? Where was I now? Would this suffocating shade of gray every change color? Would I ever care again? Would I ever hope again ? Would I ever want to live again?

I felt like I was at the bottom of a very deep, deep, well whose walls were lacquered in slippery slime. I saw no light. I saw no way out. The boulders were pushing me under, pushing me under, pushing me under. I could not breathe. I was drowning in guilt, shame, punishing myself for how others had treated me badly and of course, for how I had treated others badly too. Punishing whips, suffocating boulders, evil voices chanting: "no one wants you around, it is true there is nothing good in you".

Choice to Live

Life is made up of a series of everyday choices we make, and each one has an everlasting impact on our lives, and the lives of everyone and everything around us. I am so eternally grateful for my eldest son, who called every day to ask me how I was, to check in on me. Most times, all I had to say was negative for all I saw was how bad I was, and I wanted to blame the world for my darkness. So when he lovingly would ask "how was your day" my response was mostly a long list of complaints. I truly do not know how he endured these hopeless conversations without wanting to just hang up on me and never call again. His Love was my life raft. His call was a moment where I knew I was thought of and cared for. His call was a ray of hope, a spark of light.

One night, about four years into this horrifying existence, for everyone, he called and told me Truths I needed to hear, and was ready to hear. "Mom, we all love you so much. We have tried so many things to help you get better, but until you want to live, no matter how much we love you, things are not going to change. Mom, we have respected your request to not have ECT again, and yet, that is all that is left to try. I know you don't like it Mom, and yet to get well sometimes we must do things we do not like. Think of Aunt Claire, do you think she likes Chemotherapy ?…". Those words of Truth opened a part of me that needed to be opened. I lay in my bed for the first time in so long, thinking of someone other than myself. I thought this child has called me every day, people have done so much to try and make me better, so many in so many ways, and yet, the Truth was it was all up to me and my choices. I really did not want to have ECT again, yet I had to for my children, for my husband, for all those who had given so much of themselves for me. I had to try, to give something back for all the love of so many. I had to think of someone other than myself, and in that moment, I decided to do ECT again, really for my children, for I still did not care at all about myself. The love of so many, especially my husband and our three sons, gave me reason to live again.

ECT

❖

A treatment where you lay on a table, and probes are put all around your head to send electricity to put you in a convulsive state. Doctors really do not know why this treatment has such success with people who are in major depression, like me, yet they know it has a very high success rate. I have my ideas as to how and why, but that is for another day and another book. What is incredible, is after the fourth treatment, I knew something had shifted, something was different inside of me.

It was a gorgeous June day, crystal blue skies and warm sunshine. I stepped out of my husband's car and started walking to my apartment. I felt lighter somehow and I thought maybe I could wash my hair. I had not washed for years, for water felt like glue to me, but this day I thought maybe it would be different. I got a towel, some shampoo and went to the kitchen sink to see. When I put my head under the faucet, for the first time in years the water felt wonderful, and washing my hair was the first step of a million, that has brought me to this moment to write my story. It was such an exciting moment, for I knew the darkness was lifting, shifting, changing, and I could feel a ray of hope. I truly feel it was a miracle, the miracle of the power of Love.

One Step at a Time

The first step in washing my hair was the first of so many now. I have learned life is lived one moment at a time. One choice at a time. One step at a time. I have learned the process of healing. I learned I needed to feel what was inside of me to release it. I needed to feel the rip tide of pain that my mothers story ended so differently than mine. There was no miracle where she chose life again, at least, not here on earth. She did take her life at the age of fifty four years old. I lost my Mom when I was twenty three years old, and my heart needed to feel the pain of so many experiences that were terrifying, so many experiences that seemed impossible to understand, so many experiences that I needed to forgive, let go of. So many beliefs that God's Truth and Love has shifted. I was brought out of this great darkness to learn what is the light.

Each and every day is filled with new understanding of Love, new understanding of what is True. I have learned the power of Truth, that it is what sets us free. I have learned there are so many Truths I did not want to see or feel and yet as I do, I am becoming more loving and more free, it is a beautiful ride.

Most importantly, and amazingly, the blocks to God's Love are being healed. While I had loved God for many years and longed for Her Love, my belief that I was unworthy and unlovable blocked the experience of Her Divine Love. I believed in God and I believed Love was all we needed, yet I had not experienced its Truth yet. I had not experienced God's Love and Truth until I was willing to be completely honest with myself about how I really felt inside. I discovered I really did not believe in Love and I really did not have True Hope. Why?

I had to come face to face with the Truth that what I believed was love was not possible. That I really had no idea what love really was. That I had spent my life trying to earn love, when in Truth love can never be earned for it is a gift given to be treasured. I had spent my life trying to please others so that they would love me and in the process completely lost myself.

I have a sense of gratitude I have never experienced before. The gratitude that others' prayers and love in action saved me, gave me another chance to live my life again. Each day is a treasured gift of learning, growing, feeling, healing, dancing, laughing, crying, sharing, writing, painting, and praying....

I am now connected to my heart and all the loving angels and guides teaching me how to learn what love is, and how to love myself. Now when my eldest son calls and asks about my day, I share what a good day it is. I worked with my amazing counselor again, who I had worked with for many years. I learned to tell people when they hurt me, and most especially I felt and knew that God and all Her Angels were always with me guiding and loving me every step of the way.

I no longer believe in God, I now have an intimate relationship with Her. God has become my very best friend for She is the one who created me and in the one Being in the universe who Loves me perfectly. She is the one who is teaching me the beautiful grace of forgiveness and repentance. My heart is now wide open and vulnerable to each and every moment, for I know they are perfectly orchestrated for my soul's healing and growth.

I am letting go of my rage and anger and feeling deep bone grief for all the ways others did not love me and all the ways I did not love others. Each day is full of such deep joy, for I know for certain, there is a Loving Divine Creator who longs for us to heal and grow in Divine Love and live in eternal bliss. God's design is Utopia, and each of us has the opportunity to experience Her Truth and Love each and every day.

My hope and prayer is for everyone to experience these Truths and live in their spark every moment and always.

PEACE JOY LOVE
ALWAYS

Thoughts & Reflections
How To Support Someone Who Is Depressed

The first thing I want to say is we all are unique and have had our own individual experiences, so each person will have their own very one of a kind experience of depression. However, there are some common experiences and truths for anyone who is suffering from depression that I would like to share from what I have learned through my experience.

Firstly, as most psychologists already understand, depression is caused by the person turning their anger towards themselves, as they say, "anger turned inward". It is very True that anger, and in fact, rage, is the root of depression. It is also True that depression is the result of NOT wanting to actually feel these feelings. There are many reasons why we choose to punish ourselves, blame ourselves, rather than face the Truth of our experiences. Many of us are taught by our parents to punish ourselves, when we do not behave as they want us to. Many of us are told that they are loving us when they punish us. Many of us are taught that anger is bad and unloving, and we are bad if we are angry, thus we suppress it. Many of us have had absolutely no role models for how to experience our feelings in a safe and healing way. So as children, when our parents get angry and punish us, we often blame ourselves and thus the spiral of self punishments begins.

Depression is actually a state where we are trying so hard to NOT feel our shadow side, our darker painful emotions. The problem is, the soul can not just isolate certain feelings and feel others. When we are suppressing massive feelings of anger, fear and grief, we are using all our life force to go against what our soul wants us to do to heal. Our soul is designed to feel everything. Our soul is designed to heal when we feel. Anger is always an emotion we use to not feel the fear or grief which is underneath it. Anger is an emotion we use to control others with. Anger is an emotion that is telling us there is something that is unhealed inside of us, and needs our loving attention. The bigger the anger, the deeper the hurt.

Someone who is depressed has learned to not feel their True feelings and instead punish themselves. Someone who is depressed often has decided to give up, not try any more for they believe all their efforts will only result in another failure. I wonder if those of us who find ourselves in the landscape of depression are really trying to hide from their True feelings inside of themselves of feeling like a failure, of feeling unworthy, of feeling not good enough? Could it be that in their childhood that is how they felt and how they learned to think of themselves? Could it be that depression is not so much a genetic issue as an issue of family patterns of not knowing how to feel their feelings? Could it be that we are so afraid of our feelings, that we choose not to give them any space to express themselves? Could it be that our culture actually believes feelings are what creates our suffering and pain, when in Truth it is our disconnection to our feelings that is what actually causes our suffering and pain. Could it be that all the ways we learned to hide from our feelings, lie about our feelings, pretend we do not have these feelings are what bring us to the experience of hopelessness, despair, and the desire to not feel anymore?. The desire to not live anymore? Could it be that the source of our life lives in our feelings, passions and desires, which we have learned to not allow ourselves to experience?

I can only speak to my experience and hope it may help others. What I needed most, was someone who understood I had so much anger, rage, fear and grief inside of me that I needed to feel. I needed someone who would be honest with me, with a kind and compassionate heart. I needed someone to tell me only I could feel these feelings I was trying so hard to hide and run away from, in my self punishing addiction. That these feelings I had been holding onto since my childhood were in much need of healing. I needed someone to understand and tell me, I was not to blame for my experience, but I was responsible for healing it, for only I could feel in order to heal. I needed someone to understand that I had been taught to blame myself for others unloving choices, and that I needed to learn to love myself, and part of loving myself meant I needed to stop punishing myself, and instead open my heart to feel the rage that I was suppressing. To feel the rage at my father for abandoning my mother in her darkest hour, for lying and manipulating, all for his favor. I had to feel the gut wrenching grief that my Mother, who was my favorite person in my life, took her life, when I was twenty three. I had to feel how hard it was that I was given the responsibility of being my mothers care caretaker at the age of eleven, and that I was actually angry about it. I had to open my heart and feel the many moments of trauma in my mothers manic episodes.

I feel one of the most important things for anyone who is trying to help someone who is depressed is to understand they can not make them better. They can not take their pain away. In fact, the most loving thing they can do is to encourage them to open their hearts and feel it. Encourage them to express this rage inside of themselves. Explain to them that when they are open to this rage, fear and grief it will be an overwhelmingly emotional experience for awhile, but they will be healing their heart and soul and more joy and beautiful feelings and experience will take its place. I think it is very important to be very honest with compassion. Tell them that by not allowing themselves to feel these painful feelings they are hurting themselves and in fact, everyone around them. They must come to understand that no one else can do this for them, even the ones who created the hurt in the first place. They must understand that as long as they hold onto this anger, fear, and grief they will never be free and joyous, as God designed them to be. They also need to understand their soul is designed to heal itself through the process of feeling. That in fact, their soul will grow into a more beautiful kind being if they do. It is Truth with Love that will enable them to feel and to heal. Remind them that God is always with them and always loving them, and they can pray to ask God to help them feel these feelings they are so afraid to feel. To remind them they are never alone, no matter how alone they may feel. That they have a loving guide who is there to show them the way to joy, and eternal bliss, for that is God's design and intention.

Most of all I needed prayer and compassion. I needed someone who was not trying to fix me, but instead, trying to help me understand me. I did not need medication which everyone tried to force on me. I did not need people to tell me what to do and how to do it. I needed compassion, understanding, and kindness. Most of all, I needed to be told I had a lot of anger, a lot of grief that I was trying not to feel. I needed someone to tell me I had to start being honest with myself.

Most of all I needed prayer. I needed someone to tell me that there was a Being who already loved me perfectly and surely. That I had an angel with me always who could teach me about how to learn to love myself. That I was allowed to feel my anger, express it without hurting anyone else, including myself. I needed to be assured that I would be able to let these feelings go by feeling them, and in fact, the only way I was ever going to let them go was to have the courage and desire to feel them. I needed to understand that depression is caused by a huge desire to not feel, which actually shuts down the soul, which needs to feel to be healthy and alive.

There are many degrees of depression, I was in a "major depressive" cycle. Truth was I did not want to live anymore. I felt like no matter how much I tried in life, I always failed, so why care anymore? I felt I really was a failure, for my mother had taken her life and my husband had left me. I believed if I was a better person, none of this would have happened to me. I had learned to blame myself for others choices, rather than feel the Truth they did not love me, which of course felt really bad.

I did not need to be viewed and analyzed as someone who was sick, but rather, as someone who had massive pain to feel. I needed someone who really wanted to understand, instead of wanting to fix. As a caretaker I believe we all must understand the most loving choice is to be with someone where they are and ask them what they want to do, never forcing any decision. We must be willing to let go of trying to fix them and instead love them where they are.

There were many people trying to help me, yet most of them had agendas for what I needed. I needed a safe place to open my heart and soul again. I needed to take responsibility for these feelings I had been running from all my life.

I had a woman who came to be with me each day to bring me on walks to get me out etc. She was a wonderful, kind and loving person. We did yoga together, crocheting and even a little cooking. All these efforts were so kind and loving, yet I was avoiding what I had to face.

Truth is many tried to help in all so many ways. What I have learned though is I had given up, I did not want to live anymore and yet here I am writing a book about finding my spark and keeping it.

Prayer is the answer. Prayer in action. I was so blessed, for I had a son who called me every day. A son who told me things I needed to hear. A son who brought me out to eat, even though I had not showered or bathed in literally years. A son who did not give up on me. His call was my life raft, for I knew someone loved me, someone cared. That call was prayer in action. That call was love in action. That call, and all his Truth I needed to hear, saved me.

Truly I know it was prayer that saved me. It was God and all Her Angels that saved me. It was my son's love in action that saved me. It was my ex-husbands love in action that saved me. Most of all it was God's Love and Grace that saved me.

My hope and prayer is that anyone suffering with depression can come to understand that the despair they are feeling is real, for this world is in a very unloving and very dark condition. However, the beautiful Truth is Real Love is always around us. We each have spiritual guides and guardians who are trying to communicate with us, and teach us the Truth of God, of God's Design, and Laws, all of which are created to teach us all that Love is Real and our True Home.

Opening My Heart

We each have to discover the best way to communicate and express all our feelings. I have found writing to be like a life raft to me, as well as, painting, poetry, playing piano, hiking, camping, traveling, gardening, dancing, and singing. These are all ways I am learning to express myself and connect more deeply to myself.

I decided to include some of the poetry I wrote and paintings I made during these last three almost four years of overwhelming healing graces. I have learned the gift of forgiveness and repentance that heal and purify my soul and bring new life and joy into each and every day.

I encourage you to find your ways to heal. Listen to your heart and your guides. Allow yourself to connect more deeply to all the parts of you, even the most painful ones that are longing to be healed.

Full Circle

Life is full circle

Full of wonder
Full of joy
Full of endings and
New beginnings

Nothing is ever lost
Only transformed ...

Life is a
Full circle
Gift of
Love...

I Pray

One day
You will know
How much you
Are
LOVED

By God
By Me

I Pray

One day
I will know
How much I
Am
LOVED

By God
By You

I Pray

We Are Meant To Be…

It Is Time

To live my dreams...
To write my books...
To share my heart ...

It Is Time...

To Forgive My Past
To treasure the silver linings
To Let Go of demands, expectations & attachments.
To be open and humble in every moment.
To learn in my experience.
To feel each moment fully.

It Is Time

To stand up for Truth
To seek Forgiveness rather than Justice
To Plant my Faith in Love instead of Fear

It is Time.

To Let My Light Shine....

JOY

Singing
Swaying
Swirling

Celebrating
Spirals

Glistening
Transforming
Opening

Dapples of
Light
Laughing

Listening

I will listen
to the language
of my life
Accepting the syntax
of my present
experience
No clinging to
what could have
been or
what will be
I will feel fully
allow my
experience
to break me
wide open
empty me
transforming the
language of
my experience
into the Alphabet of Grace

Stop Running

Stand
Still
Wide
Open

Feel
Each
Moment
Fully

Grateful
For
Each
Breath

Let Go
Let Go
Let Go

Fly
Free...

In
Divine
Embrace

The River

Polish the stones of
My living
Into dazzling
Landscapes

Open my soul
In
Budding
Blossom

Heal
With
Your lapping
Songs of
LOVE

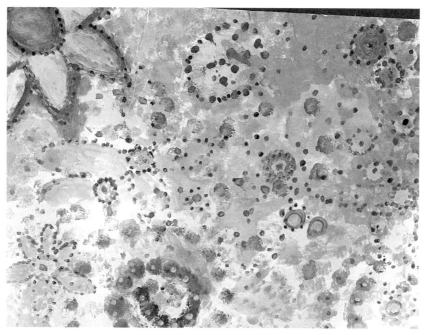

Afterword

I have found in my life that there really is no past, present or future those are constructs we create to understand our experiences, indeed, life is full circle. I have come to understand that the past always lives in the present and births the future. I have also learned that if we do not heal the wounds of our past, they are certain to bleed into our everyday experience and not only hurt ourselves but also so many innocent others that are connected in our life, most especially our partners and children. I have come to understand so many things through my experience with our Divine Creator.

Many people have asked me how I came from such darkness into such light? I wrote this story in an attempt to answer that question for myself and any others that are interested. My hope and prayer is that my story brings hope to another who may be in their moment of darkness, that it will bring hope to those loved ones who are so desperate to help, and yet have no idea just how.

My experience taught me the Truth I Always believed in, that Love is All You Need. My experience taught me what True Love is, so much more than a fleeting feeling or our codependent addictions. My experience taught me the power of prayer. My experience taught me that from great darkness, great light can be born, if we want it to.. My experience taught me that each of our lives is orchestrated in a Divine Love that lives and moves and breaths in our every moment. My experience teaches me every day that we are all always loved so deeply, surely and perfectly we just must learn to believe …

My experience taught me the power of simple kindness., the cruelness of judgement, and that Divine Love is the most powerful energy in the universes.. My experience taught me the power and grace of forgiveness. My experience taught me deep bone compassion. I learned we are all interconnected and when we hurt another we hurt ourselves. My experience taught me how important it is that we stop living in our walls of self protection, for they keep are hearts rigid in the fear they are trying to protect. And so sadly, it is our rigid hearts born in fear, that create our unloving choices and unloving desires. When we live in fear, we compete, we are jealous, we believe we are better than another, or conversely, like me, we believe we are worse than another, we believe all our lies and then spray them all over those we claim to "love". So sadly, on planet earth we really have not learned what love is yet. I believe with all my being, that the only True Way to Peace on Earth, Goodwill towards men, is each one of us will stop looking at our facade with great approval as Narcissist did, and start looking at ourselves through the lens of Divine Truth and Divine Love and allow the Holy Ones to help us purify and soften our hearts into flesh. If we each did, war would not exist, betrayal would not exist, adulatory would not exist, jealousy would not exist, arrogance would not exist, competition would not exist...It would be a world that God Always Desires for us to create. A world where everyone would treasure the gift that their life is. A world where everyone would be the unique beautiful creation God created them to be. Where each person would know they are loved without condition. Where each person would really understand when they hurt another, they hurt themselves. Where each person would be one hundred percent responsible for their choices and the resulting consequences. Where people would STOP blaming others for their unkindness., and choose to always be kind. Where everyone would Love God and be grateful for their lives as the gift that they are.

This short memoir, my little life experiences, led me to the Absolute Truth of God and Gratitude for all Her Loving Creations. My blocks to Love have been healed, and each and every day Divine Love purifies and heals my soul, actually, is transforming it into a new creation. This is why I am certain, I have found My Spark and it will always grow brighter and brighter each and every day.

My hope and prayer is that everyone will find their spark and let it shine.

PEACE. JOY. LOVE. ALWAYS

About The Author

Margaret currently lives in Maryland. Her experience includes a 35 year marriage and raising three wonderful sons, one of her greatest life joys. She has created and facilitated Sacred Listening Groups when she worked at Hospice in graduate school. She also wrote and published her first book "Sacred Listening From Fear To Love" in 2012. Now, ten years later she has written and published "Finding My Spark and Keeping It".

Margaret has many interests and passions. She is currently, designing a Healing Arts Center which will include, music, drama, writing, dancing, and the fine arts. This dream is currently a desire she prays will manifest soon. Her greatest joy is watching her three sons blossom and bloom. Margaret, loves to hike, camp, travel, write, play music, dance, sing, and support and encourage others on their healing journey. Her first love is God who has become her very best friend. She puts prayer and her faith as the most important things in her life. She is learning that what Jesus said two thousand years ago, and continues to teach is so very True; "put God first and all things shall be handed unto you".

If you want to contact Margaret her website is sacredlisteninghealing.com, where you can gain access to some radio and tv interviews as well as some articles she has written.

Printed in the United States
by Baker & Taylor Publisher Services